Password
Book

Name : ....

Email : ....

Phone: ....

Password Log

Website	
Name	
Username	
Email	
Password / pin	
Notes	

— ❧ — — ❧ — — ❧ — — ❧ —

Website	
Name	
Username	
Email	
Password / pin	
Notes	

— ❧ — — ❧ — — ❧ — — ❧ —

Website	
Name	
Username	
Email	
Password / pin	
Notes	

Password Log

Website	
Name	
Username	
Email	
Password / pin	
Notes	

- - ✦ - - ✦ - - ✦ - - ✦ -

Website	
Name	
Username	
Email	
Password / pin	
Notes	

- - ✦ - - ✦ - - ✦ - - ✦ -

Website	
Name	
Username	
Email	
Password / pin	
Notes	

Password Log

Website	
Name	
Username	
Email	
Password / pin	
Notes	

Website	
Name	
Username	
Email	
Password / pin	
Notes	

Website	
Name	
Username	
Email	
Password / pin	
Notes	

Password Log

Website	
Name	
Username	
Email	
Password / pin	
Notes	

Website	
Name	
Username	
Email	
Password / pin	
Notes	

Website	
Name	
Username	
Email	
Password / pin	
Notes	

Password Log

Website	
Name	
Username	
Email	
Password / pin	
Notes	

Website	
Name	
Username	
Email	
Password / pin	
Notes	

Website	
Name	
Username	
Email	
Password / pin	
Notes	

Password Log

Website	
Name	
Username	
Email	
Password / pin	
Notes	

Website	
Name	
Username	
Email	
Password / pin	
Notes	

Website	
Name	
Username	
Email	
Password / pin	
Notes	

Password Log

Website	
Name	
Username	
Email	
Password / pin	
Notes	

— ❧ — — ❧ — — ❧ — — ❧ —

Website	
Name	
Username	
Email	
Password / pin	
Notes	

— ❧ — — ❧ — — ❧ — — ❧ —

Website	
Name	
Username	
Email	
Password / pin	
Notes	

Password Log

Website	
Name	
Username	
Email	
Password / pin	
Notes	

— ✺ — — ✺ — — ✺ — — ✺ —

Website	
Name	
Username	
Email	
Password / pin	
Notes	

— ✺ — — ✺ — — ✺ — — ✺ —

Website	
Name	
Username	
Email	
Password / pin	
Notes	

Password Log

Website	
Name	
Username	
Email	
Password / pin	
Notes	

Website	
Name	
Username	
Email	
Password / pin	
Notes	

Website	
Name	
Username	
Email	
Password / pin	
Notes	

Password Log

Website	
Name	
Username	
Email	
Password / pin	
Notes	

Website	
Name	
Username	
Email	
Password / pin	
Notes	

Website	
Name	
Username	
Email	
Password / pin	
Notes	

Password Log

Website	
Name	
Username	
Email	
Password / pin	
Notes	

— ✦ — — ✦ — — ✦ — — ✦ —

Website	
Name	
Username	
Email	
Password / pin	
Notes	

— ✦ — — ✦ — — ✦ — — ✦ —

Website	
Name	
Username	
Email	
Password / pin	
Notes	

Password Log

Website	
Name	
Username	
Email	
Password / pin	
Notes	

Website	
Name	
Username	
Email	
Password / pin	
Notes	

Website	
Name	
Username	
Email	
Password / pin	
Notes	

Password Log

Website	
Name	
Username	
Email	
Password / pin	
Notes	

Website	
Name	
Username	
Email	
Password / pin	
Notes	

Website	
Name	
Username	
Email	
Password / pin	
Notes	

Password Log

Website	
Name	
Username	
Email	
Password / pin	
Notes	

— ❧ — — ❧ — — ❧ — — ❧ —

Website	
Name	
Username	
Email	
Password / pin	
Notes	

— ❧ — — ❧ — — ❧ — — ❧ —

Website	
Name	
Username	
Email	
Password / pin	
Notes	

Password Log

Website	
Name	
Username	
Email	
Password / pin	
Notes	

Website	
Name	
Username	
Email	
Password / pin	
Notes	

Website	
Name	
Username	
Email	
Password / pin	
Notes	

Password Log

Website	
Name	
Username	
Email	
Password / pin	
Notes	

Website	
Name	
Username	
Email	
Password / pin	
Notes	

Website	
Name	
Username	
Email	
Password / pin	
Notes	

Password Log

Website	
Name	
Username	
Email	
Password / pin	
Notes	

Website	
Name	
Username	
Email	
Password / pin	
Notes	

Website	
Name	
Username	
Email	
Password / pin	
Notes	

Password Log

Website	
Name	
Username	
Email	
Password / pin	
Notes	

Website	
Name	
Username	
Email	
Password / pin	
Notes	

Website	
Name	
Username	
Email	
Password / pin	
Notes	

Password Log

Website	
Name	
Username	
Email	
Password / pin	
Notes	

Website	
Name	
Username	
Email	
Password / pin	
Notes	

Website	
Name	
Username	
Email	
Password / pin	
Notes	

Password Log

Website	
Name	
Username	
Email	
Password / pin	
Notes	

—⁓⁓— —⁓⁓— —⁓⁓— —⁓⁓—

Website	
Name	
Username	
Email	
Password / pin	
Notes	

—⁓⁓— —⁓⁓— —⁓⁓— —⁓⁓—

Website	
Name	
Username	
Email	
Password / pin	
Notes	

Password Log

Website	
Name	
Username	
Email	
Password / pin	
Notes	

Website	
Name	
Username	
Email	
Password / pin	
Notes	

Website	
Name	
Username	
Email	
Password / pin	
Notes	

Password Log

Website	
Name	
Username	
Email	
Password / pin	
Notes	

Website	
Name	
Username	
Email	
Password / pin	
Notes	

Website	
Name	
Username	
Email	
Password / pin	
Notes	

Password Log

Website	
Name	
Username	
Email	
Password / pin	
Notes	

Website	
Name	
Username	
Email	
Password / pin	
Notes	

Website	
Name	
Username	
Email	
Password / pin	
Notes	

Password Log

Website	
Name	
Username	
Email	
Password / pin	
Notes	

Website	
Name	
Username	
Email	
Password / pin	
Notes	

Website	
Name	
Username	
Email	
Password / pin	
Notes	

Password Log

Website	
Name	
Username	
Email	
Password / pin	
Notes	

— ꕥ — — ꕥ — — ꕥ — — ꕥ —

Website	
Name	
Username	
Email	
Password / pin	
Notes	

— ꕥ — — ꕥ — — ꕥ — — ꕥ —

Website	
Name	
Username	
Email	
Password / pin	
Notes	

Password Log

Website	
Name	
Username	
Email	
Password / pin	
Notes	

Website	
Name	
Username	
Email	
Password / pin	
Notes	

Website	
Name	
Username	
Email	
Password / pin	
Notes	

Password Log

Website	
Name	
Username	
Email	
Password / pin	
Notes	

— ❦ — — ❦ — — ❦ — — ❦ —

Website	
Name	
Username	
Email	
Password / pin	
Notes	

— ❦ — — ❦ — — ❦ — — ❦ —

Website	
Name	
Username	
Email	
Password / pin	
Notes	

Password Log

Website	
Name	
Username	
Email	
Password / pin	
Notes	

— — — — — — — —

Website	
Name	
Username	
Email	
Password / pin	
Notes	

— — — — — — — —

Website	
Name	
Username	
Email	
Password / pin	
Notes	

Password Log

Website	
Name	
Username	
Email	
Password / pin	
Notes	

Website	
Name	
Username	
Email	
Password / pin	
Notes	

Website	
Name	
Username	
Email	
Password / pin	
Notes	

Password Log

Website	
Name	
Username	
Email	
Password / pin	
Notes	

Website	
Name	
Username	
Email	
Password / pin	
Notes	

Website	
Name	
Username	
Email	
Password / pin	
Notes	

Password Log

Website	
Name	
Username	
Email	
Password / pin	
Notes	

Website	
Name	
Username	
Email	
Password / pin	
Notes	

Website	
Name	
Username	
Email	
Password / pin	
Notes	

Password Log

Website	
Name	
Username	
Email	
Password / pin	
Notes	

— ❦ — — ❦ — — ❦ — — ❦ —

Website	
Name	
Username	
Email	
Password / pin	
Notes	

— ❦ — — ❦ — — ❦ — — ❦ —

Website	
Name	
Username	
Email	
Password / pin	
Notes	

Password Log

Website	
Name	
Username	
Email	
Password / pin	
Notes	

Website	
Name	
Username	
Email	
Password / pin	
Notes	

Website	
Name	
Username	
Email	
Password / pin	
Notes	

Password Log

Website	
Name	
Username	
Email	
Password / pin	
Notes	

Website	
Name	
Username	
Email	
Password / pin	
Notes	

Website	
Name	
Username	
Email	
Password / pin	
Notes	

Password Log

Website	
Name	
Username	
Email	
Password / pin	
Notes	

Website	
Name	
Username	
Email	
Password / pin	
Notes	

Website	
Name	
Username	
Email	
Password / pin	
Notes	

Password Log

Website	
Name	
Username	
Email	
Password / pin	
Notes	

— ❧ — — ❧ — — ❧ — — ❧ —

Website	
Name	
Username	
Email	
Password / pin	
Notes	

— ❧ — — ❧ — — ❧ — — ❧ —

Website	
Name	
Username	
Email	
Password / pin	
Notes	

Password Log

Website	
Name	
Username	
Email	
Password / pin	
Notes	

Website	
Name	
Username	
Email	
Password / pin	
Notes	

Website	
Name	
Username	
Email	
Password / pin	
Notes	

Password Log

Website	
Name	
Username	
Email	
Password / pin	
Notes	

Website	
Name	
Username	
Email	
Password / pin	
Notes	

Website	
Name	
Username	
Email	
Password / pin	
Notes	

Password Log

Website	
Name	
Username	
Email	
Password / pin	
Notes	

Website	
Name	
Username	
Email	
Password / pin	
Notes	

Website	
Name	
Username	
Email	
Password / pin	
Notes	

Password Log

Website	
Name	
Username	
Email	
Password / pin	
Notes	

Website	
Name	
Username	
Email	
Password / pin	
Notes	

Website	
Name	
Username	
Email	
Password / pin	
Notes	

Password Log

Website	
Name	
Username	
Email	
Password / pin	
Notes	

— ✑ — — ✑ — — ✑ — — ✑ —

Website	
Name	
Username	
Email	
Password / pin	
Notes	

— ✑ — — ✑ — — ✑ — — ✑ —

Website	
Name	
Username	
Email	
Password / pin	
Notes	

Password Log

Website	
Name	
Username	
Email	
Password / pin	
Notes	

— ✦ — — ✦ — — ✦ — — ✦ —

Website	
Name	
Username	
Email	
Password / pin	
Notes	

— ✦ — — ✦ — — ✦ — — ✦ —

Website	
Name	
Username	
Email	
Password / pin	
Notes	

Password Log

Website	
Name	
Username	
Email	
Password / pin	
Notes	

Website	
Name	
Username	
Email	
Password / pin	
Notes	

Website	
Name	
Username	
Email	
Password / pin	
Notes	

Password Log

Website	
Name	
Username	
Email	
Password / pin	
Notes	

— ❧ — — ❧ — — ❧ — — ❧ —

Website	
Name	
Username	
Email	
Password / pin	
Notes	

— ❧ — — ❧ — — ❧ — — ❧ —

Website	
Name	
Username	
Email	
Password / pin	
Notes	

Password Log

Website	
Name	
Username	
Email	
Password / pin	
Notes	

Website	
Name	
Username	
Email	
Password / pin	
Notes	

Website	
Name	
Username	
Email	
Password / pin	
Notes	

Password Log

Website	
Name	
Username	
Email	
Password / pin	
Notes	

Website	
Name	
Username	
Email	
Password / pin	
Notes	

Website	
Name	
Username	
Email	
Password / pin	
Notes	

Password Log

Website	
Name	
Username	
Email	
Password / pin	
Notes	

Website	
Name	
Username	
Email	
Password / pin	
Notes	

Website	
Name	
Username	
Email	
Password / pin	
Notes	

Password Log

Website	
Name	
Username	
Email	
Password / pin	
Notes	

Website	
Name	
Username	
Email	
Password / pin	
Notes	

Website	
Name	
Username	
Email	
Password / pin	
Notes	

Password Log

Website	
Name	
Username	
Email	
Password / pin	
Notes	

Website	
Name	
Username	
Email	
Password / pin	
Notes	

Website	
Name	
Username	
Email	
Password / pin	
Notes	

Password Log

Website	
Name	
Username	
Email	
Password / pin	
Notes	

Website	
Name	
Username	
Email	
Password / pin	
Notes	

Website	
Name	
Username	
Email	
Password / pin	
Notes	

Password Log

Website	
Name	
Username	
Email	
Password / pin	
Notes	

Website	
Name	
Username	
Email	
Password / pin	
Notes	

Website	
Name	
Username	
Email	
Password / pin	
Notes	

Password Log

Website	
Name	
Username	
Email	
Password / pin	
Notes	

Website	
Name	
Username	
Email	
Password / pin	
Notes	

Website	
Name	
Username	
Email	
Password / pin	
Notes	

Password Log

Website	
Name	
Username	
Email	
Password / pin	
Notes	

Website	
Name	
Username	
Email	
Password / pin	
Notes	

Website	
Name	
Username	
Email	
Password / pin	
Notes	

Password Log

Website	
Name	
Username	
Email	
Password / pin	
Notes	

— ✑ — — ✑ — — ✑ — — ✑ —

Website	
Name	
Username	
Email	
Password / pin	
Notes	

— ✑ — — ✑ — — ✑ — — ✑ —

Website	
Name	
Username	
Email	
Password / pin	
Notes	

Password Log

Website	
Name	
Username	
Email	
Password / pin	
Notes	

Website	
Name	
Username	
Email	
Password / pin	
Notes	

Website	
Name	
Username	
Email	
Password / pin	
Notes	

Password Log

Website	
Name	
Username	
Email	
Password / pin	
Notes	

— ✦ — — ✦ — — ✦ — — ✦ —

Website	
Name	
Username	
Email	
Password / pin	
Notes	

— ✦ — — ✦ — — ✦ — — ✦ —

Website	
Name	
Username	
Email	
Password / pin	
Notes	

# Password Log

Website	
Name	
Username	
Email	
Password / pin	
Notes	

Website	
Name	
Username	
Email	
Password / pin	
Notes	

Website	
Name	
Username	
Email	
Password / pin	
Notes	

Password Log

Website	
Name	
Username	
Email	
Password / pin	
Notes	

Website	
Name	
Username	
Email	
Password / pin	
Notes	

Website	
Name	
Username	
Email	
Password / pin	
Notes	

Password Log

Website	
Name	
Username	
Email	
Password / pin	
Notes	

Website	
Name	
Username	
Email	
Password / pin	
Notes	

Website	
Name	
Username	
Email	
Password / pin	
Notes	

Password Log

Website	
Name	
Username	
Email	
Password / pin	
Notes	

Website	
Name	
Username	
Email	
Password / pin	
Notes	

Website	
Name	
Username	
Email	
Password / pin	
Notes	

Password Log

Website	
Name	
Username	
Email	
Password / pin	
Notes	

Website	
Name	
Username	
Email	
Password / pin	
Notes	

Website	
Name	
Username	
Email	
Password / pin	
Notes	

Password Log

Website	
Name	
Username	
Email	
Password / pin	
Notes	

Website	
Name	
Username	
Email	
Password / pin	
Notes	

Website	
Name	
Username	
Email	
Password / pin	
Notes	

Password Log

Website	
Name	
Username	
Email	
Password / pin	
Notes	

— ✷ — — ✷ — — ✷ — — ✷ —

Website	
Name	
Username	
Email	
Password / pin	
Notes	

— ✷ — — ✷ — — ✷ — — ✷ —

Website	
Name	
Username	
Email	
Password / pin	
Notes	

Password Log

Website	
Name	
Username	
Email	
Password / pin	
Notes	

Website	
Name	
Username	
Email	
Password / pin	
Notes	

Website	
Name	
Username	
Email	
Password / pin	
Notes	

Password Log

Website	
Name	
Username	
Email	
Password / pin	
Notes	

Website	
Name	
Username	
Email	
Password / pin	
Notes	

Website	
Name	
Username	
Email	
Password / pin	
Notes	

Password Log

Website	
Name	
Username	
Email	
Password / pin	
Notes	

Website	
Name	
Username	
Email	
Password / pin	
Notes	

Website	
Name	
Username	
Email	
Password / pin	
Notes	

Password Log

Website	
Name	
Username	
Email	
Password / pin	
Notes	

Website	
Name	
Username	
Email	
Password / pin	
Notes	

Website	
Name	
Username	
Email	
Password / pin	
Notes	

Password Log

Website	
Name	
Username	
Email	
Password / pin	
Notes	

Website	
Name	
Username	
Email	
Password / pin	
Notes	

Website	
Name	
Username	
Email	
Password / pin	
Notes	

Password Log

Website	
Name	
Username	
Email	
Password / pin	
Notes	

Website	
Name	
Username	
Email	
Password / pin	
Notes	

Website	
Name	
Username	
Email	
Password / pin	
Notes	

Password Log

Website	
Name	
Username	
Email	
Password / pin	
Notes	

Website	
Name	
Username	
Email	
Password / pin	
Notes	

Website	
Name	
Username	
Email	
Password / pin	
Notes	

Password Log

Website	
Name	
Username	
Email	
Password / pin	
Notes	

Website	
Name	
Username	
Email	
Password / pin	
Notes	

Website	
Name	
Username	
Email	
Password / pin	
Notes	

Password Log

Website	
Name	
Username	
Email	
Password / pin	
Notes	

— ⸙ — — ⸙ — — ⸙ — — ⸙ —

Website	
Name	
Username	
Email	
Password / pin	
Notes	

— ⸙ — — ⸙ — — ⸙ — — ⸙ —

Website	
Name	
Username	
Email	
Password / pin	
Notes	

Password Log

Website	
Name	
Username	
Email	
Password / pin	
Notes	

Website	
Name	
Username	
Email	
Password / pin	
Notes	

Website	
Name	
Username	
Email	
Password / pin	
Notes	

Password Log

Website	
Name	
Username	
Email	
Password / pin	
Notes	

— ⸂⸃ — — ⸂⸃ — — ⸂⸃ — — ⸂⸃ —

Website	
Name	
Username	
Email	
Password / pin	
Notes	

— ⸂⸃ — — ⸂⸃ — — ⸂⸃ — — ⸂⸃ —

Website	
Name	
Username	
Email	
Password / pin	
Notes	

Password Log

Website	
Name	
Username	
Email	
Password / pin	
Notes	

Website	
Name	
Username	
Email	
Password / pin	
Notes	

Website	
Name	
Username	
Email	
Password / pin	
Notes	

Password Log

Website	
Name	
Username	
Email	
Password / pin	
Notes	

Website	
Name	
Username	
Email	
Password / pin	
Notes	

Website	
Name	
Username	
Email	
Password / pin	
Notes	

Password Log

Website	
Name	
Username	
Email	
Password / pin	
Notes	

Website	
Name	
Username	
Email	
Password / pin	
Notes	

Website	
Name	
Username	
Email	
Password / pin	
Notes	

Password Log

Website	
Name	
Username	
Email	
Password / pin	
Notes	

Website	
Name	
Username	
Email	
Password / pin	
Notes	

Website	
Name	
Username	
Email	
Password / pin	
Notes	

Password Log

Website	
Name	
Username	
Email	
Password / pin	
Notes	

Website	
Name	
Username	
Email	
Password / pin	
Notes	

Website	
Name	
Username	
Email	
Password / pin	
Notes	

Password Log

Website	
Name	
Username	
Email	
Password / pin	
Notes	

Website	
Name	
Username	
Email	
Password / pin	
Notes	

Website	
Name	
Username	
Email	
Password / pin	
Notes	

Password Log

Website	
Name	
Username	
Email	
Password / pin	
Notes	

Website	
Name	
Username	
Email	
Password / pin	
Notes	

Website	
Name	
Username	
Email	
Password / pin	
Notes	

Password Log

Website	
Name	
Username	
Email	
Password / pin	
Notes	

— ∽∾ — — ∽∾ — — ∽∾ — — ∽∾ —

Website	
Name	
Username	
Email	
Password / pin	
Notes	

— ∽∾ — — ∽∾ — — ∽∾ — — ∽∾ —

Website	
Name	
Username	
Email	
Password / pin	
Notes	

Password Log

Website	
Name	
Username	
Email	
Password / pin	
Notes	

Website	
Name	
Username	
Email	
Password / pin	
Notes	

Website	
Name	
Username	
Email	
Password / pin	
Notes	

Password Log

Website	
Name	
Username	
Email	
Password / pin	
Notes	

Website	
Name	
Username	
Email	
Password / pin	
Notes	

Website	
Name	
Username	
Email	
Password / pin	
Notes	

Password Log

Website	
Name	
Username	
Email	
Password / pin	
Notes	

Website	
Name	
Username	
Email	
Password / pin	
Notes	

Website	
Name	
Username	
Email	
Password / pin	
Notes	

Password Log

Website	
Name	
Username	
Email	
Password / pin	
Notes	

— — — — — — — —

Website	
Name	
Username	
Email	
Password / pin	
Notes	

— — — — — — — —

Website	
Name	
Username	
Email	
Password / pin	
Notes	

Password Log

Website	
Name	
Username	
Email	
Password / pin	
Notes	

— ✦ — ✦ — ✦ — ✦ —

Website	
Name	
Username	
Email	
Password / pin	
Notes	

— ✦ — ✦ — ✦ — ✦ —

Website	
Name	
Username	
Email	
Password / pin	
Notes	

Password Log

Website	
Name	
Username	
Email	
Password / pin	
Notes	

— ⊂⊱⊰⊃ — — ⊂⊱⊰⊃ — — ⊂⊱⊰⊃ — — ⊂⊱⊰⊃ —

Website	
Name	
Username	
Email	
Password / pin	
Notes	

— ⊂⊱⊰⊃ — — ⊂⊱⊰⊃ — — ⊂⊱⊰⊃ — — ⊂⊱⊰⊃ —

Website	
Name	
Username	
Email	
Password / pin	
Notes	

Password Log

Website	
Name	
Username	
Email	
Password / pin	
Notes	

Website	
Name	
Username	
Email	
Password / pin	
Notes	

Website	
Name	
Username	
Email	
Password / pin	
Notes	

Password Log

Website	
Name	
Username	
Email	
Password / pin	
Notes	

Website	
Name	
Username	
Email	
Password / pin	
Notes	

Website	
Name	
Username	
Email	
Password / pin	
Notes	

Password Log

Website	
Name	
Username	
Email	
Password / pin	
Notes	

Website	
Name	
Username	
Email	
Password / pin	
Notes	

Website	
Name	
Username	
Email	
Password / pin	
Notes	

Password Log

Website	
Name	
Username	
Email	
Password / pin	
Notes	

Website	
Name	
Username	
Email	
Password / pin	
Notes	

Website	
Name	
Username	
Email	
Password / pin	
Notes	

Password Log

Website	
Name	
Username	
Email	
Password / pin	
Notes	

Website	
Name	
Username	
Email	
Password / pin	
Notes	

Website	
Name	
Username	
Email	
Password / pin	
Notes	

Password Log

Website	
Name	
Username	
Email	
Password / pin	
Notes	

Website	
Name	
Username	
Email	
Password / pin	
Notes	

Website	
Name	
Username	
Email	
Password / pin	
Notes	

Password Log

Website	
Name	
Username	
Email	
Password / pin	
Notes	

Website	
Name	
Username	
Email	
Password / pin	
Notes	

Website	
Name	
Username	
Email	
Password / pin	
Notes	

Password Log

Website	
Name	
Username	
Email	
Password / pin	
Notes	

Website	
Name	
Username	
Email	
Password / pin	
Notes	

Website	
Name	
Username	
Email	
Password / pin	
Notes	

Password Log

Website	
Name	
Username	
Email	
Password / pin	
Notes	

— ✦ — — ✦ — — ✦ — — ✦ —

Website	
Name	
Username	
Email	
Password / pin	
Notes	

— ✦ — — ✦ — — ✦ — — ✦ —

Website	
Name	
Username	
Email	
Password / pin	
Notes	

Password Log

Website	
Name	
Username	
Email	
Password / pin	
Notes	

Website	
Name	
Username	
Email	
Password / pin	
Notes	

Website	
Name	
Username	
Email	
Password / pin	
Notes	

Password Log

Website	
Name	
Username	
Email	
Password / pin	
Notes	

— ⟋⟍ — ⟋⟍ — ⟋⟍ — ⟋⟍ —

Website	
Name	
Username	
Email	
Password / pin	
Notes	

— ⟋⟍ — ⟋⟍ — ⟋⟍ — ⟋⟍ —

Website	
Name	
Username	
Email	
Password / pin	
Notes	

Password Log

Website	
Name	
Username	
Email	
Password / pin	
Notes	

Website	
Name	
Username	
Email	
Password / pin	
Notes	

Website	
Name	
Username	
Email	
Password / pin	
Notes	

Password Log

Website	
Name	
Username	
Email	
Password / pin	
Notes	

— ❧ — — ❧ — — ❧ — — ❧ —

Website	
Name	
Username	
Email	
Password / pin	
Notes	

— ❧ — — ❧ — — ❧ — — ❧ —

Website	
Name	
Username	
Email	
Password / pin	
Notes	

Password Log

Website	
Name	
Username	
Email	
Password / pin	
Notes	

Website	
Name	
Username	
Email	
Password / pin	
Notes	

Website	
Name	
Username	
Email	
Password / pin	
Notes	

Password Log

Website	
Name	
Username	
Email	
Password / pin	
Notes	

Website	
Name	
Username	
Email	
Password / pin	
Notes	

Website	
Name	
Username	
Email	
Password / pin	
Notes	

Password Log

Website	
Name	
Username	
Email	
Password / pin	
Notes	

Website	
Name	
Username	
Email	
Password / pin	
Notes	

Website	
Name	
Username	
Email	
Password / pin	
Notes	

Password Log

Website	
Name	
Username	
Email	
Password / pin	
Notes	

Website	
Name	
Username	
Email	
Password / pin	
Notes	

Website	
Name	
Username	
Email	
Password / pin	
Notes	

Password Log

Website	
Name	
Username	
Email	
Password / pin	
Notes	

Website	
Name	
Username	
Email	
Password / pin	
Notes	

Website	
Name	
Username	
Email	
Password / pin	
Notes	